GREAT MALE DANCERS

ERIK BRUHN

GREAT
MALE DANCERS

by

CYRIL SWINSON

ADAM AND CHARLES BLACK

LONDON

FIRST PUBLISHED 1964
BY A. & C. BLACK LTD
4, 5 & 6 SOHO SQUARE
LONDON W.1

PREFACE

CYRIL SWINSON was working on this book before his last illness, and the uncompleted manuscript was found among his papers after his death in January 1963. Happily the greater part was in a finished state, and much of the rest was in draft. Only the final section on the English dancers was unwritten, but his rough notes gave an indication of his plan and I have endeavoured to complete the work as I believe he would have done.

IVOR GUEST

MADE IN GREAT BRITAIN
PRINTED BY MORRISON AND GIBB LIMITED, LONDON AND EDINBURGH

"IT is a pity that you can't find a better title than *Great Male Dancers*," I was told when this book was first suggested. "Isn't there a masculine equivalent of *ballerina* or something?" "The masculine of the Italian *ballerina*," I explained, "is *baollerin*, and nowadays it is rarely used, even in Italy."

What other term can be used instead of "great male dancers"? In France at the Paris Opéra, the home of ballet, a principal male dancer is known as *un premier danseur*, and if he is outstanding he may be elevated by the Director to be an *étoile*, and described on the programme as *un danseur étoile*. In Russia, where the roots of ballet may be traced back to the foundation of the Imperial Theatre School by the Empress Anne in 1738, there are grades similar to those in Paris, through which a dancer must progress, before he reaches the highest rank. Thereafter his, or more frequently her, position in the ballet hierarchy is indicated by the honours awarded by a constituent republic of the Soviet Union, or, an even greater distinction, by the Central Government of the U.S.S.R. Thus Galina Ulanova and other senior ballerinas are designated People's Artists of the U.S.S.R. Senior male dancers in the Bolshoi Theatre, such as Yuri Zhdanov, Alexander Lapauri and Nicolai Fadeyechev, have the lesser distinction of Honoured Artist of the R.S.F.S.R. In Denmark, where ballet has had royal patronage since 1748, the Royal Danish Ballet lists its principal dancers merely as *Solodancers*. Only on the rarest occasion are dancers elevated above this, and it was not until 1942 that the Royal Danish Ballet, for the first time in its history, nominated a *prima ballerina*. Margot Lander received this signal honour, and in the same year Børge Ralov was similarly honoured when he was nominated *First Solodancer*.

In England The Royal Ballet has reduced its main grades of dancers to three : the *corps de ballet*, soloists and artists or principal dancers, who are listed, however great their claims to fame, in strict alphabetical order. There was a time when Robert Helpmann's name was displayed alongside and even before Margot Fonteyn's. The title given him, even if it was unofficial, was principal male dancer.

Ballet companies which are not state subsidised rarely have official rankings, and the names of the dancers are displayed in an order determined by the management, a difficult task which rarely gives satisfaction, except to the dancers appearing at the head of the list. (A former ballerina of the New York City Ballet, which lists its principal dancers in the same way as The Royal Ballet, is reported to have said that while she did not mind being *listed* alphabetically, she would not be *treated* alphabetically.)

Occasionally a male dancer's name precedes all others. Thus, when Anton Dolin was a member of London's Festival Ballet, his name appeared at the head of the list of dancers, and although he danced infrequently, it was understandable that it should. Similarly when Igor Youskevitch was with the American Ballet Theatre his name appeared before all others.

This dissertation has not helped to discover a suitable alternative title for this small book, but at least it has revealed that on two or three occasions in recent years the eminence or fame of the principal male dancer in a company was held to be more important in the eyes of the management than its ballerinas. A principal male dancer and a ballerina do not, however, achieve greatness by the position of their names on the company's roster or their official ranking. Erik Bruhn, for instance, appeared at the end of the list of ten *solodancers*, when the Royal Danish Ballet visited London in 1953, since he was the most junior, but in the minds of all who saw him during the company's short season, there was no doubt at all that he was the finest artist of them all.

Danseur noble is a term often used to describe a dancer with a noble classical style. Bruhn is a great *danseur noble*, so was Michael Somes, but it is not essential for every great male dancer to be *un danseur noble*. Alexander Grant and Rudolf Nureyev are not *danseurs nobles* but both, in different ways, are great dancers.

Before an attempt is made to suggest who are some of the great male dancers of to-day, and to assess the qualities which distinguish a very good, or even a brilliant dancer, from a great one, it is important to emphasise that the male dancer is an indispensable part of ballet. Whenever this has been forgotten, as it was in the Romantic period of ballet in the nineteenth century, ballet has declined. Indeed, it has been said that " if Russia had not safeguarded and preserved the male dancer when France was making his position artistically intolerable, ballet would have died ! " *

Ballet, as we know it to-day, began long before the Romantic Ballet. In the sixteenth century it was an amusement and a pastime for the

* Arnold L. Haskell : *Ballet Panorama* (Batsford).

Apollon —— *Le Roy*

6   LOUIS XIV AS APOLLO IN A COURT BALLET OF 1654

Photo: Bibliothèque de l'Institut, Paris

courtiers of the several principalities and grand duchies of Italy and in France where Catherine de Medici, mother of the young kings, Charles IX and Henri III, encouraged her sons to take an active part in the ballets of the court, so that she could concern herself with matters of state. Henri IV, an active dancer himself, had his son, later Louis XIII, taught dancing from an early age. With such royal patronage and active participation, ballet at the French court flourished, as it did at almost every other royal court in Europe.

Ballet, at this time, was exclusively an entertainment for the court, and new and elaborate ballets were produced for almost every important occasion. In France the King and the Queen frequently danced in the ballets, and not unnaturally the courtiers developed a passion for ballet which rivalled their royal masters. Bassompière, the great Marshal of France, for example, was such a devotee, that he used ballet terms for his military commands. When he was about to storm a fortress, his final word of command was, " The *décor* and the dancers are ready : now the ballet can begin."

The court ballets often had for their theme some aspect of power or majesty, and emphasised the semi-divine nature of kingship. In 1653, Louis XIV appeared as the Sun King (le Roi soleil) in the *Ballet de la Nuit*. He was then fifteen years of age, but already an accomplished dancer, having made his début in ballet, in *Cassandre* two years previously. His love of dancing and court entertainment exceeded that of all other French kings, and when growing corpulence and preoccupation with more serious matters made it impossible for him to continue dancing himself, he made arrangements for ballet to continue without royal participation, and ensured that there would always be an adequate supply of trained dancers.

First, he founded in 1661 the Académie Royale de Danse, which consisted of a council of thirteen dancing masters, whose object was to maintain " the art of dance in its perfection." Ten years later he founded the Académie Royale de Musique, and from this organisation has descended the Paris Opéra Ballet of to-day.

With Louis XIV's retirement as a dancer, the courtiers began to play a less active part in ballet, although a high standard of dancing was still considered to be an essential part of a courtier's education. The King himself had said that the art of dancing was one of the most useful arts for the nobility, " not only in wartime in the army, but also in peacetime in the *divertissements* of our ballets." With the withdrawal of the king, professional dancers began to take over.

The production of the court ballets had always been in the hands of professional musicians, and the first task of the Académie Royale de Danse in 1661 was to codify the court dances and character dances, and to ensure that they would be correctly taught to the professional dancers who would eventually succeed the courtiers. Twenty years later, in 1681, after Louis XIV had given permission for an opera house to be opened in Paris, so that the public at large could witness performances, professional dancers were still few in number. For the presentation in Paris of the ballet *Le Triomphe de L'Amour*, which had been given at court four months previously, the King was asked to allow certain courtiers to appear in the Paris production. They were allowed to do so " without losing their rank." When the ballet had been presented at court Charles Beauchamps had danced the feminine rôle, but in Paris the part was danced by Mlle. Lafontaine, the first professional woman dancer whom the history of ballet records. Previously all the women's rôles had been danced by the Queen or the ladies of the court, or *en travesti*. (Louis XIII appeared more than once, and with great success, as an old woman.)

At first the professional dancers recruited by Beauchamps (who was not only a brilliant dancer, but a choreographer and the first director of the school of dancing attached to the Académie Royale de Musique) were tumblers and acrobats who appeared at fairs, and Beauchamps had to obtain the King's permission before he was allowed to train them. But in 1681, although Beauchamps was able to provide not only Mlle. Lafontaine, but also a number of other *danseuses* from the Académie, there were still insufficient dancers for all the parts.

Opera and ballet soon became increasingly popular with the public in Paris, and early in the eighteenth century a school of dance was established at the Paris Opéra to ensure a continuous supply of trained dancers. Technique was still limited, by to-day's standards, but from Feuillet's *Chorégraphie*, first published in 1700, it is possible to see the basis from which the technique of classical ballet was later developed. The technical terms, many of which survive to-day, included *cabrioles*, *coupés*, *chassés*, *entrechats* and *sisonnes*. Many of these steps were at first performed only by male dancers, and indeed it would have been impossible for women, in their long full skirts to attempt any quick steps or movements. The man's costume, which at first was the conventional court dress with knee breeches and heeled shoes, gave him a freedom of movement denied to the *danseuse*. Thus, the male dancer, at this time, far outshone the

COSTUME DESIGNED FOR GAÉTAN VESTRIS IN
THE MIDDLE OF THE EIGHTEENTH CENTURY

woman. Beauchamps himself, Louis Pécour and
Jean Balon were all great dancers of the period.
Balon had such an extraordinary lightness of
movement that it is not impossible that the term
ballon, meaning springiness or elasticity of the
feet, is derived from his name. He was said to
be the greatest dancer in Europe, and, a rare
distinction, he was permitted to shake the King,
Louis XIV, by the hand.

The next great dancer was Louis Dupré, who
was known as " le grand Dupré " and " the God
of the Dance." Male supremacy in the dance
was lessened a little by Camargo. A pupil of
Pécour, Blondy (a nephew of Beauchamps, and
a distinguished dancer) and of Dupré, she quickly
established herself as a favourite with the Paris
public. By shortening her long skirts a few inches
she was able to perform steps which no woman
had performed in Paris before. Praising Camargo,
Voltaire said that she was the first woman to dance
like a man. Marie Sallé was another dancer
who won great popularity, but for sheer technique
a young Italian dancer, Barberina, astonished

audiences at the Opéra by performing *entrechats
huit*. Camargo's feat of performing *entrechats
quatre* seemed relatively easy by comparison.

The success of these three dancers was a slight
setback to male supremacy in the dance, but men
still dominated the stage. The greatest male
dancer of this period was Gaétan Vestris. A pupil
of Dupré, and a great *danseur noble*, like his master
he was also called the God of the Dance. Vestris's
son, Auguste, was another great dancer. It says
much for the father that he acknowledged that
the only dancer greater than himself was his son.
Auguste excelled as a *demi-caractère* dancer, the
equivalent of an Alexander Grant of to-day. The
two Vestris had an unparalleled success, and
when, for instance, father and son were dancing
in London in 1781, a sitting of Parliament was
suspended to allow the Members to attend at the
opera house. A rival of Auguste, in his later
years, was Louis Duport, who was exceptional for the ease and grace of his movements.
" Although this was an age when the male
dancer was king," Ivor Guest writes in *The
Dancer's Heritage*,* " there were many famous
ballerinas too . . . But gifted though they were,
these ballerinas were often overshadowed by the
brilliance of a Vestris or a Duport." But the end
of this age of supremacy was at hand, and a few
years later the virtuosity of the ballerina dealt a
blow to the art of ballet and to male dancing
from which it has never fully recovered.

Two typical ballets of the eighteenth century
are *Les Indes Galantes*, first produced in 1735, and
La Fille Mal Gardée (1789). *Les Indes Galantes* was
an opera-ballet in a prologue and four *entrées*,
and it was a most spectacular production, making
use of an army of singers and dancers and with
elaborate scenic effects. It was revived at the
Paris Opéra in 1952, when it again achieved a
great popular success. Its theme was the triumph
of love over violence and war, and it drew heavily
upon mythology for the various episodes. *La Fille
Mal Gardée* was one of the first ballets to break
away from mythology. The gods and goddesses,
and the symbolic creatures to be found in the
ballets of the court and in later periods, have no
place in its simple story of country life. A new
version of the ballet created by Frederick Ashton
in 1960 follows the original story, and Ashton's
changes would appear to be largely in the
choreography and the tempo of many of the
dances. But the ballet itself shows clearly that
the principal male dancer's rôle is as important
to the development of the story as the ballerina's.

This balance changed slowly in the early years
of the nineteenth century, but with the coming
of the Romantic Ballet, the balance rose to the
highest point in the ballerina's favour.

* Published A. & C. Black Ltd., 1960.

For a study of the Romantic movement and its influence on ballet the reader must be referred to the many admirable histories of ballet available. Our concern here is with the male dancer. In the first of the great Romantic ballets *La Sylphide* (1832) there is a mixture of earthly and ethereal elements. The young Scots lad, James, is bewitched upon the eve of his wedding by a sylph, a mysterious fairy-like creature, who flies unseen in and out of the assembling wedding guests. James deserts his bride and goes in pursuit of the sylph. A witch tells him how to entrap her, but when he does, her wings drop from her shoulders and she dies, to be borne heavenwards by ingenious stage machinery. The Sylph is typical of most of the Romantic heroines, and Marie Taglioni, who created the rôle, seemed to have been born for it. Her sharp, elfin-like features and her lyrical dancing with its lightness and graceful leaps had an element of poetry. Her dancing on *pointe* emphasised her remoteness from merely *terre à terre* movements. Although she had not been the first dancer to dance on *pointe*, she was certainly the first to use it to extend her art. Others had merely used it as a feat.

The introduction of dancing on *pointe* was one of the greatest and most important developments in the technique of ballet. Until the end of the eighteenth century heeled shoes had been in general use, but with the removal of the heels the dancer was able to move more swiftly and lightly. To achieve the appearance of added lightness, the dancer could raise her heels off the ground, and when her shoes were padded and she learned to move on *pointe*, choreographers were not slow to use this new means of expression. The simplification of the dancer's costume gave her as much freedom of movement as the male dancer already enjoyed, and this led to other developments in technique, and to new movements devised by choreographers.

The rôle of James in *La Sylphide* was an important one, but of less importance than the ballerina's. In *Giselle* (1841), the best known of all the Romantic ballets, Albrecht's rôle is again important, but can be overshadowed by the part of Giselle herself. The first Giselle was Carlotta Grisi, and Albrecht was Lucien Petipa, a great dancer of his time, and then more famous than his brother Marius.

The success of *La Sylphide* stimulated a new interest in the ballet, and poets, painters and writers were inspired by the exquisite dancing of Taglioni and the ballerinas who succeeded her in their affections. In the many charming lithographs of the period the emphasis, understandably, is always on the beauty and grace of the ballerina. In the writings of the period, there is

AUGUSTE VESTRIS

the same emphasis. Théophile Gautier (1811–72), the most prominent of the critics, has eyes only for the ballerina, and very rarely indeed does the *corps de ballet* receive a mention. His comments on the male dancer give an indication of his position at this time.

"Art for art's sake," was Gautier's credo. "Dancing after all has no other object but the revelation of beautiful form, in graceful attitudes and the development of lines which are agreeable to the eye." He found his ideals in Taglioni, Fanny Elssler and Carlotta Grisi, and as much as he idolised and idealised them, he despised the male dancer. "Nothing is more abominable," he writes, "than a man who displays his red neck, his great muscular arms, his legs with calves like church beadles, his whole heavy masculine frame shaken with leaps and pirouettes." One or two male dancers found favour in his eyes, but only because they kept themselves in the background, and made good partners for their ballerinas. Gautier found that the male dancers at the Paris Opéra "are of a nature to encourage the opinion which will only allow women in ballet." "They affect," he wrote, "that false grace, those ambiguous and revolting manners which has sickened the public of male dancing." He went further: "For us a male dancer is something monstrous and indecent which we cannot conceive . . . strength is the only grace permissible to men."

9

Gautier modified his opinions so far as Jules Perrot (1810–92) was concerned. Perrot was short and far from handsome, and his master Auguste Vestris had advised him to keep moving while dancing, so that the audience might not have time to see what he looked like. Gautier was enraptured by his performance in *Le Zingaro* in 1840. He asserted that he was " the greatest dancer of his time, with the torso of a tenor, and the perfect legs of a Greek statue. We do not," he went on, " in the least care for male dancing ; a man executing anything but character dances or pantomime has always seemed to us a kind of monster . . . Perrot has made us lose our prejudice." With the arrival in Paris of Arthur Saint-Léon (1821–70) several years later, Gautier once again modified his general condemnation of male dancing, and was prepared to admit the possibility of a male element in ballet, although he did not consider it necessary or even highly desirable.

Gautier's partial retraction of his views came too late. The ballets which followed *Giselle* gave decreasing opportunities for the male dancer. He could not be dispensed with entirely in the *corps de ballet* or for character parts, but in *Coppélia*, produced in Paris in 1870, the rôle of Frantz was danced *en travesti* by a woman, Eugénie Fiocre. This was the ultimate absurdity, and when Swanilda needed support, Frantz stepped back and a man from the *corps de ballet* stepped forward to hold the ballerina. By this time the supply of superlative ballerinas, from Taglioni onwards, which had nourished the ballet and made it popular, was exhausted. Ballet in Paris fell into decline, and it was many years before the decline was arrested.

In Denmark the male dancer fared better, due to August Bournonville. A great dancer and the son of a dancer, he had danced leading rôles in Paris and London before he returned to Denmark in 1829. Between 1829 and his retirement in 1877, he revitalised the Royal Danish Ballet. His style of dancing, known now as the Bournonville style, was derived largely from the French style of Vestris, and under this system Bournonville produced many virile and elegant male dancers. Three notable dancers of to-day are products of this system, Erik Bruhn, Flemming Flindt and Henning Kronstam. One of them, Erik Bruhn, who has had a wide experience of other methods of training, believes that the Bournonville method has much to offer other systems of training, and in collaboration with Lillian Moore he has written a modest book on the subject.* In the ballets he created, many of which are still in the repertoire of the Royal Danish Ballet to-day, Bournonville gave ample opportunities to the male dancers in his company. The work of the company was little known outside Denmark until recent years, but its contribution to the standard of male dancing, especially in the nineteenth century, was considerable. Christian Johansson (1817–1903), for instance, studied under Bournonville, and became *premier danseur* in St. Petersburg in 1841. He stayed on in Russia, and eventually became the chief teacher at the Imperial School in St. Petersburg, influencing considerably the formation of the Russian school of dancing. His pupils included many of those who became the brightest stars of the glorious period of Russian ballet at the end of the nineteenth century.

The Romantic ballets were introduced to Russia shortly after their first productions in Paris.

JULES PERROT

* *Bournonville and Ballet Technique* (A. & C. Black Ltd.).

ARTHUR SAINT-LÉON IN *LA ESMERALDA*

La Sylphide was presented in 1837 with Taglioni in the title-rôle. It was a great success, and *Giselle*, which followed in 1842, had an equally enthusiastic reception. Visiting ballerinas from Italy and France, and occasionally Russian ballerinas, sustained popular interest in the ballet, and the male dancer, it seems, was in much the same position as in France, with the notable exception that the strong tradition of national and regional folk dance in Russia gave more opportunities for male dancing in subordinate rôles and *divertissements* and male rôles were never danced *en travesti*. But the general decline in the popularity of ballet in Russia followed a pattern not unlike that experienced in Paris. When the supply of visiting ballerinas gave out, nothing, it seemed, could stimulate popular interest. Marius

Petipa, who had arrived in Russia in 1847 to become *premier danseur* at St. Petersburg, was appointed *maître de ballet* in 1862. He produced countless ballets, in most cases works with a romantic theme, and his sole requisite in the composition of a ballet was " that everything should be centred on one principal character to be interpreted by the *prima ballerina.*" *

Much has been written about Petipa's methods of constructing his ballets, and an examination of even one of his ballets will show indeed that everything was subordinated to the *prima ballerina*. In *Don Quichotte* (1869), with music by Ludwig Minkus, his scenario is said to be based upon Cervantes' famous novel. But the fragments of the novel taken by Petipa are only a framework on which to hang an endless series of dances

* Cyril W. Beaumont : *Complete Book of Ballets* (Putnam).

11

which contribute nothing to the development of the story. Don Quichotte himself, his faithful servant Sancho Panza and other important characters have non-dancing rôles, and the scenes in which the story is told take up possibly ten minutes. All the rest of the ballet is devoted to dancing : a great many solos for the ballerina, numerous dances and movements for the *corps de ballet* and for groups of dancers and minor characters, and finally a *pas de deux* for the heroine Kitri and her lover Basil, a barber. A revised version of the ballet was created with new choreography by Alexander Gorsky in Moscow in 1902. The Ballet Rambert produced the Gorsky version in 1962, and this production demonstrates more forcibly than by any other means the sorry state of ballet in the nineteenth century. There is no real characterisation, but only caricature ; there is no real development of the plot, the choreography is extremely limited and boringly repetitious, and its success depends almost entirely upon the abilities of the *ballerina*.

Petipa produced many other ballets after the pattern of *Don Quichotte*, and all the time the popularity of ballet declined. The poor man was at his wits' end to find new ways of attracting support for ballet. The turn of the tide came in 1881 when Ivan Vsevolojsky was appointed director of the Imperial Theatres. At first Petipa was apprehensive of the new director, and he feared that the virtual dictatorship he had enjoyed for so many years was now at an end. Petipa came to accept the changes of the new director, and in his memoirs he praises Vsevolojsky highly and frequently mentions the " unforgettable years " of their work together. One of Vsevolojsky's first moves was to arrange for the retirement of the official composer, Ludwig Minkus, who for over twenty years had been writing music for the ballet in Moscow and later in St. Petersburg. Later Vsevolojsky persuaded Tchaikovsky to compose a ballet score, and with a carefully notated list of Petipa's requirements before him, Tchaikovsky wrote the music for *The Sleeping Beauty*. Petipa, who had been accustomed to working with musical hacks who were ready to produce whatever length of music he required, realised at once the quality of Tchaikovsky's music. In the past he had often composed his dances before the music was written ; with the music for *The Sleeping Beauty* before him he was inspired, and with this ballet began the golden age of the Imperial Russian Ballet. The teachers under Petipa's direction included Christian Johansson, Enrico Cecchetti (who was still at this time a magnificent dancer himself, and created the Blue Bird and Carabosse, the wicked fairy godmother, in *The Sleeping Beauty*) and Nicholas Legat, also

a *premier danseur*, who had begun to teach in 1889. Between them they produced a magnificent company of dancers which has never been equalled. After *The Sleeping Beauty* in 1890, came *Swan Lake* and *The Nutcracker*, and these ballets, all with scores by Tchaikovsky, gave new life and popularity to ballet. But for the male dancer, his position was virtually unchanged. There were, it is true, solos for the *premier danseur*, a few character *divertissements* and national dances in the new ballets, but the ballet was still dominated by the ballerina : either by guest ballerinas from Italy or by the Imperial Ballet's own ballerinas.

A spirit of revolt stirred among a few of the dancers, and one of them, Michel Fokine, foreseeing little future for himself as a dancer, at one time contemplated resignation from the Imperial Ballet to become a painter.

Fokine had passed his final examination in the Imperial Ballet School in 1898. The examiners were headed by Marius Petipa and Paul Gerdt, who in his time had been one of the greatest *danseurs nobles* in Russian ballet, but who was now teacher of the senior class. So impressed were the examiners with Fokine's outstanding talent, that they petitioned the Director, Vsevolojsky, to take Fokine into the Company. Instead of beginning his career in the *corps de ballet*, as the regulations stipulated, Fokine was at once cast for important parts. He joined the special class for dancers given by Johansson, and his future as a dancer in the Imperial Ballet was assured. At a very early age he was appointed to teach the technique of classical ballet, first to junior girls, and later to the senior class.

In time Fokine became dissatisfied with his life as a dancer and teacher, and he came to the conclusion " that ballet had reached a point beyond which it could not advance so long as it continued to be bound by the iron rules of tradition." *

The ballets of the period, as we have briefly observed, were planned according to a stereotyped pattern, and were designed primarily for the adulation of the ballerina. But this was not all. In an Egyptian ballet while the supers would be in the costume of the period, the ballerina wore the customary tutu with jewels of her own choice and with her hair dressed *à la mode*. As a concession to the theme of the ballet she would wear possibly a lotus flower on her costume. The style of dancing, whatever the theme and setting of the ballet, was pure classical dancing ; conventional ballet gestures were used and no attempt was made to capture the correct style or atmosphere. The scenario often had no coherence or logical development. Fokine's view was that the ballet must be freed of conventional gestures

* Cyril W. Beaumont : *Michel Fokine and His Ballets.*

and costume, and the set order of steps, and above all that there must be a unity of action and a unity of style in harmony with the music, which, in its turn, must be truly expressive of the theme and setting chosen for the ballet.

He prepared a scenario for a two-act ballet, planning it in accordance with his ideas of how a ballet should be produced. He submitted it to the director of the Imperial Theatres, with explanatory notes, which included a plan for the reform of ballet.

His plan was ignored, and Fokine sought other means of trying out his ideas by producing small ballets for the annual pupils' displays and for charity performances. Although Fokine's plan for reform does not mention the male dancer and the relatively unimportant part he played in the ballets of the time, it is an inherent part of the plan. If there is unity of action in a ballet, dances will not be introduced merely to display the virtuosity of the ballerina, but will come when the action demands them. And unless the hero is a cripple in an invalid chair, his part in the ballet and his opportunities for dancing will not be restricted to partnering the ballerina with an occasional solo to give the ballerina a few minutes' rest. This is an over-simplification of the position, but if a comparison is made between the nineteenth-century *Swan Lake* and the eighteenth-century *La Fille Mal Gardée*, it is not difficult to say which of the two ballets Fokine would consider fitted into his conception of what ballet should be.

The full story of Fokine's rebellion against the traditions of the Imperial Ballet can be found in *The Dancer's Heritage* * and many other books on the ballet. Our concern is with the changed position of the male dancer as it emerged in Fokine's ballets and to note briefly the opportunities given to him by Fokine.

One of Fokine's greatest innovations was to produce short ballets of one-act duration and his early experiments of this kind included *Les Sylphides* (as it came to be called) and *Le Carnaval.*

At the time Fokine was dancing and teaching in St. Petersburg, creating his early ballets and worrying about the state of ballet in the Imperial Theatre, a young man, Serge Diaghilev, was introducing Russian art and culture to Paris. In 1906 he had presented an exhibition of Russian painting, the following year he had arranged concerts of Russian music, and in 1908 he presented a Russian opera, Moussorgsky's *Boris Godounov*, with Chaliapine as Boris. Although Diaghilev had held an official position in the Imperial Theatre for a short time, he had shown no special interest in the ballet. His modern outlook and his artistic ideas were not in sympathy

* By Ivor Guest (A. & C. Black Ltd.).

with the hidebound condition of the Imperial Ballet and he soon found himself in disagreement with his superiors, whereupon he was relieved of his post. After the success of *Boris Godounov*, Diaghilev decided he would arrange another season of opera for the following year. At the insistence of his friend Alexandre Benois, with whom he had earlier collaborated in the publication of a periodical *The World of Art*, he agreed to include ballets in his programme. Benois considered ballet an interesting art form, " which by some miracle had survived in Russia, whereas it had died out everywhere else." * At the Maryinsky Theatre at that time, as he pointed out to Diaghilev, there was a company of " exceptionally brilliant male and female dancers, including a young man named Nijinsky, who had only just completed his training. Secondly, there appeared to have dawned a new era in choreography." *

Diaghilev began to appear at performances of Fokine's ballets. His interest and enthusiasm for ballet developed rapidly, and he began to make plans for the season in Paris. He engaged Fokine as *maître de ballet*, and among his principal dancers were Pavlova, Karsavina, Fokine, Adolph Bolm, Mikhail Mordkin and Vaslav Nijinsky. The repertoire for the first Paris season consisted of *Le Pavillon d'Armide*, the *Polovtsian Dances* from *Prince Igor*, *Les Sylphides*, *Cléopâtre*, all with choreography by Fokine, and a suite of dances called *Le Festin*, which included the Bluebird *pas de deux* from *The Sleeping Beauty* (re-called for the occasion *L'Oiseau de Feu*).

The first performance of Diaghilev's Russian Ballet was 19th May 1909. It is a memorable date in ballet history for a number of reasons, but so far as we are concerned, it began a new era for the male dancer in ballet. The Parisian audience was amazed by Nijinsky's dancing and compared him with Vestris. Bolm in the part of the chief warrior in *Prince Igor* had a reception which was equally enthusiastic. Fokine's contribution to the success of the evening was not overlooked by the critics, and he was praised not only for his originality, but for the skill in which he had welded the solos into the action of the ballets, especially in *Prince Igor*, which was " saturated with such force and passion as to make of it a real *chef-d'oeuvre*." *

In describing the first appearance of the Russian dancers in Paris, I have restricted quotations to the restrained and objective account given by Serge Grigoriev, Diaghilev's *régisseur*. The critics' reports, the articles in the press, and the accounts in memoirs of the period of this first historic season in Paris would fill a volume many times the size of this small book.

* S. L. Grigoriev : *The Diaghilev Ballet 1909–1929.*

13

14

VASLAV NIJINSKY
IN *LE SPECTRE DE LA ROSE*

Maurice Goldberg

ADOLPH BOLM

It was indeed a turning of the tide for ballet, and for the male dancer. Diaghilev returned to Paris the following year, and eventually formed his own permanent company. Fokine produced a succession of new ballets (including *Schéhérazade*, *L'Oiseau de Feu*, *Le Spectre de la Rose*, *Petrushka*, *Thamar* and *Daphnis and Chloe*), in all of which the male dancers had outstanding opportunities of displaying their talents. The classical ballets of the nineteenth century found little place in Diaghilev's repertoire in the early years of his company : a short version of *Lac des Cygnes* was given in 1911, and in the previous year a revival of *Giselle*, which even Karsavina and Nijinsky failed to make a popular success.

Diaghilev was not an artist in the accepted sense of the word. He did not paint, or write, or compose, and it is said that when someone asked him what he did, he replied, "I look after the lighting." But he was, there can be no doubt, a great creative artist and co-ordinator of other people's talents. He assembled around him an intimate circle of painters, musicians, writers and critics, and occasionally a dancer, and under Diaghilev's skilful direction they discussed end-lessly new ideas and projects for ballets. The choreographer was not, as he is to-day, the most important figure in the creation of a new work. Eventually Fokine resigned from the company and Diaghilev let him go. It is possible that Diaghilev had come to the conclusion that Fokine's contribution to the art of ballet was now exhausted, and it is true that in the remaining thirty years of his life Fokine produced no new works which equal the ballets of his early inspiration.

Diaghilev was always searching, in the way in which every genuinely creative artist searches, for new ideas and new means of expression. His search led him to various branches of modern art including cubism and expressionism. He only once returned to the classical ballet of his youth, when he revived *The Sleeping Beauty* in 1921. But though, for the most part, he spurned the classical ballets, he always maintained the high stand-ards of classical technique which these ballets demanded. From his company he would select male dancers whom he thought could be de-veloped into choreographers. Nijinsky was the

below : LEONIDE MASSINE
IN *LA BOUTIQUE FANTASQUE*

first, and after his departure there was the young and brilliant Leonide Massine, who produced several outstanding ballets, including *Les Femmes de Bonne Humeur, La Boutique Fantasque* and *Le Tricorne*, before he too departed from Diaghilev's company. These ballets continued the tradition inaugurated by Fokine, so far as the male dancer is concerned : none of them are vehicles to display merely the technical virtuosity of a ballerina and they all include many opportunities for the male dancer.

Several years later a young Irish dancer, Anton Dolin, joined the company and although he developed into a brilliant virtuoso dancer and a superb partner, he did not develop, as Diaghilev had hoped, into a choreographer. Another promising young dancer of this period encouraged by Diaghilev was Serge Lifar, who became after Diaghilev's death, choreographer and *maître de ballet* at the Paris Opéra.

Diaghilev's search for new choreographers was vital for the continuing success, and indeed the existence, of his company, and there were at least four new ballets every season, except when war or other disasters, such as lack of finance, interfered with his plans. In the twenty years of his company's existence, there were many outstanding male dancers in the company at one time or another. Apart from those already noted must be mentioned Alexander Volinine, who later became a celebrated teacher in Paris, and Leon Woizikovski, a Polish dancer of immense vitality and superb in character rôles such as the Polovtsian Chief in *Prince Igor*. Stanislas Idzikowski, also a Polish dancer, joined Diaghilev in 1914, and his elevation and technique was comparable with Nijinsky's. He danced in 1933 with the Vic-Wells Ballet in London where he has taught successfully many generations of dancers. Other outstanding dancers included Pierre Vladimiroff, who danced Prince Charming in *The Sleeping Beauty* in 1921, and later partnered Pavlova ; and Anatole Vilzak, who joined Diaghilev's company in 1921, and, after Diaghilev's death, danced many important rôles in de Basil's Russian Ballet. Georges Balanchine, already an experienced dancer when he joined Diaghilev in 1925, became his last great choreographer.

One great figure in Diaghilev's company was Enrico Cecchetti. Born in Rome in 1850, he was not only one of the greatest male dancers of his time, but one of the greatest teachers in the whole history of ballet. All the dancers of the Diaghilev era passed through his hands, and when in turn many of them became teachers they carried on the strict and rigorous training without which it is not possible to produce dancers of the highest calibre.

MIKHAIL GABOVITCH IN *TARAS BULBA*

VAKHTANG CHABUKIANI
IN *THE CORSAIR*

With Diaghilev's death in 1929, his dancers were dispersed. Some found employment eventually in other companies, notably Colonel de Basil's which was first formed in 1932. Lifar went to the Paris Opéra and eventually Balanchine went to the U.S.A. Others settled down to teaching.

* * *

In Russia after Diaghilev's departure, ballet went on as before, under Imperial patronage until the Revolution, and then, with scarcely a break, under the Soviet régime. The magnificent system of training which produced the finest dancers in the world continued and indeed expanded. To-day there are more than thirty large companies throughout the U.S.S.R. Fokine's innovations found little place under the Soviet régime, although in the 'twenties new acrobatic elements found their way into Russian dancing, and greater advantage was taken of the strong folk-dance tradition in various regions of the State. But classicism held the field and is now immovably entrenched. In the repertoires of the numerous companies the nineteenth-century classics and similar new ballets predominate. All but one of the thirty companies have *Swan Lake* in their repertoire, most of them have *Giselle*, and there are over a dozen productions of *The Sleeping Beauty*. Old warhorses such as *Don Quichotte* and *La Bayadere*, both with music by Minkus, Pugni's *Esmeralda*, Adam and Delibes' *Le Corsaire*,

GEORGI FARMANYANTZ IN *ROMEO AND JULIET*

Tchaikovsky's *The Nutcracker*, and Glazounov's *Raymonda*, and twentieth-century replicas such as Asafiev's *The Fountain of Bakhchiserai*, predominate in the repertoires. There are relatively few one-act ballets, and the " revolutionary " ballet *The Red Flower* (formerly *The Red Poppy*) is in less than a dozen repertoires. The position of the male dancer in Russia would appear to be much the same as it was at the turn of the century, but from the evidence we have seen when Soviet companies have visited Western Europe, this is not the case. Conventional mime has largely disappeared, many of the old classics have been revised and now have a libretto which is more logically developed and more theatrically satisfying. The male heroes are no longer merely *porteurs* with an occasional solo. They have, as they have always had, a superb technique and they act with such force, nobility and complete sincerity that they are no longer the paste-board princes to which we have grown accustomed in the classical ballets. To character rôles, and to the *corps de ballet*, they bring the same dynamic qualities, and within the restrictions of the nineteenth-century ballets they do much to restore the balance between the sexes. Soviet ballets are no longer completely dominated by the ballerina. In the new ballets which are now being produced, both full-length and one-act works, it would appear that more opportunities are now being given to the male rôles. Vakhtang Chabukiani,

ALEXANDER LAPAURI

NICOLAI FADEYECHEV AND NADIA NERINA
IN *GISELLE*

for a long period the greatest male dancer in the Soviet Union, is now in charge of the ballet company in his native Tiflis, and concentrating on direction and choreography. If a choreographer has himself been a great dancer, as were Bournonville, Fokine and Massine, it usually follows that the male dancer's rôles in his ballets offer exceptional opportunities. Among the great male dancers seen in Western Europe or the U.S.A. must be included Yuri Zhdanov, Alexander Lapauri, Nicolai Fadeyechev, Vladimir Semenov, Yuri Soloviev, Georgi Farmanyantz and Yuri Kondratov. Of these, Fadeyechev and Soloviev were particularly admired for their elegant style and strong technique. Fadeyechev was first seen in London dancing with the Bolshoi Ballet in 1956, and his partnership with Ulanova in *Giselle* has happily been recorded on film by Dr. Paul Czinner. Soloviev, a representative of the more refined Leningrad school, headed the Kirov Ballet on its visit to London in 1961. In contrast to them, Farmanyantz is renowned as a character dancer, possessing the compact build, strength and resilience which are so ideally suitable for such parts as jesters. The list could be extended indefinitely, so many fine and promising male dancers are there in the Soviet companies.

YURI SOLOVIEV
AND ALLA SIZOVA
IN *THE STONE FLOWER*

20

Anthony Crickmay

Mydtskov

BØRGE RALOV AND KIRSTEN RALOV
IN *NAPOLI*

Among the soloists and *corps de ballet* of the Royal Danish Ballet in 1953 were two young men, Flemming Flindt and Henning Kronstam, who have since achieved international distinction for the outstanding quality of their dancing. Among the ballet children appearing in *Napoli* were Niels Kehlet and Jorn Madsen, both of whom are now *solodancers* in the company, and are already dancers of considerable achievement.

below : FLEMMING FLINDT
IN *ETUDES*

Von Haven Presse

Although its work was little known outside Denmark until after World War II, the Royal Danish Ballet has produced, under the Bournonville tradition, many outstanding, and some great, male dancers. When the company first visited England in 1953, the great Børge Ralov was, alas, forty-five, but still magnificent in the Bournonville ballet *Napoli*, Fredbjørn Bjørnsson was in his prime and dancing magnificently, and there were also Niels Bjørn Larsen, a fine dancer now concentrating on character parts, Frank Schaufuss, a dancer of great precision and charm, and above all Erik Bruhn, who conquered critics and audiences alike by the perfection of his dancing, his fine presence and his very personable good looks. Since then Bruhn has emerged as an international star of the first order, and is to be counted among the few greatest male dancers performing to-day. He left the Royal Danish Ballet in 1955 to dance with Ballet Theatre, and more recently has appeared as guest artist with The Royal Ballet at Covent Garden. This experience outside his native Denmark has been of great value to him in widening his horizon as an artist, and should he ever return permanently to Copenhagen, he may well give Danish ballet an impetus of which it has long been in need.

Mydtskov

Mydtskov

Fred Brommett

MICHEL RENAULT
IN *PRINCE IGOR*

—this is the substance of an explanation expounded in his *Traité de la danse académique*. While his technique was never in the virtuoso class, nevertheless he could transform gestures and movements, which were not themselves exceptional, into moments of rare beauty. He had the quality, which in a great actor is called "presence," and which has been called * "the 'genius' of dancing." His body was beautifully proportioned, with the narrow waist and broad shoulders of the athlete, and with his strongly individual features his personality on the stage was compelling. When he first joined the Opéra another great dancer, Serge Peretti, was already

* *A Dictionary of Modern Ballet :* Francis Gadan and Robert Maillard (Methuen).

below : PETER VAN DIJK

Rama

At the Paris Opéra Serge Lifar has been the dominating figure, with short breaks, for more than thirty years. His first ballet *Le Renard* was created very near the end of the life of Diaghilev's company in 1929, and later the same year the first of his many ballets for the Paris Opéra was presented. Our concern here is with his dancing. While his elevation was excellent, it was not exceptional. Lifar has offered an explanation, and here it should be noted that probably no other dancer or choreographer in the history of ballet, except Noverre, has written so much about his art, analysed it at such length, or propounded so many theories about technique and other aspects of the dance, as Lifar. " It is not so important to jump very high, as to give the impression that the jump lasts for a long time "

there. He was a true *danseur noble*, with " an impeccably clean and brilliant style, who could afford to underline his perfect mastery with a touch of irony " * In 1941 he received the title of *étoile*. When the Paris Opéra Ballet visited London in 1954, two other *étoiles* were admired : Michel Renault and Youly Algaroff. Renault had a meteoric career in his youth and was nominated *premier danseur étoile* in 1947 at the age of eighteen. His strong technique, allied to his dazzling charm and spirited personality, endeared him to Parisian audiences. Algaroff, already an accomplished dancer when he joined the company in 1953, is an outstanding *danseur noble*. Alexandre Kalioujny was a notable addition to the *étoiles* in 1947. A former athletic champion of Paris, his powerful technique, his strength and vigour brought to the Paris Opéra " the bravura of the Russians of the golden age." * Peter van Dijk, born in Bremen 1929, became an *étoile* at the Opéra in 1954, joining the Opéra after considerable experience with other companies. He is a fine classical dancer, elegant, reserved and with

* *A Dictionary of Modern Ballet* : Francis Gadan and Robert Maillard (Methuen).

Right : JEAN BABILÉE IN *LE JEUNE HOMME ET LA MORT* (Photo : Lipnitkzi)

Below : ROLAND PETIT AND ZIZI JEANMAIRE IN *CARMEN* (Photo : British Lion Films Ltd.)

a strong stage presence. Jean-Paul Andréani, who also became an *étoile* in 1954, is another pupil of Peretti. He has exceptional elevation and a notable technique. He made ballet history at the Paris Opéra in 1950, when he danced the rôle of Frantz in *Coppélia*, the first man to dance the rôle there, where (as we have already noted) the part had always been danced by a woman. Other male *étoiles* at the Opéra now include Attilio Labis and Flemming Flindt from the Royal Danish Ballet. It is significant of the state of male dancing in France that so many of the *étoiles* at the Paris Opéra are not products of its school. In fairness, though, it should be noted that two at least of the French male dancers of international reputation were trained at the Opéra : Roland Petit and Jean Babilée. In the immediate post-war years Petit's performance as a dancer, with his elegance, his noble carriage, his long slim legs and his pale face, was not yet overshadowed by his talents as choreographer. Babilée was not outstanding for his classical technique, although he danced with complete success rôles such as Albrecht in *Giselle*, and in *Le Spectre de la Rose*. His stage personality was magnetic, he moved with feline grace, and he had the rare gift of establishing immediately and most forcibly the complex characters of such rôles as the Joker in *Jeu de Cartes* and the young man in *Le Jeune Homme et la Mort*. Like Petit, he was a great loss to ballet, when his gifts and talents were diverted into other branches of the theatre.

* * *

Paris, since the First World War, has been a veritable hot-house of ballet. There will be found in the studios of the great teachers who work there, girls and boys of many nations. When de Basil was forming his first company in the early 'thirties, he discovered in Preobrajenska's studio the young Tamara Toumanova, Irina Baronova and Tatiana Riabouchinska, and in Egorova's studio David Lichine. Lichine was then twenty-two and had already danced in Ida Rubinstein's company and with Pavlova's company, and under de Basil he quickly emerged as a leading dancer and one of the most outstanding of his generation. Elegant, graceful, with dark handsome good looks, he danced classical rôles and created many notable parts in new ballets, including the hero in *Les Présages* and the King of the Dandies in *Le Beau Danube*. He remained with de Basil's company until 1940–41, and thereafter concentrated on teaching, choreography, and producing in various parts of the world new versions of *Graduation Ball* and his other successful ballets. In de Basil's company for a long period was Yurek Shabalevsky, a Polish dancer of immense charm, precision and attack. His performances with the company in

YUREK SHABALEVSKY
IN *CONCURRENCE*

Maurice Seymour

IGOR YOUSKEVITCH
IN *THE BLACK SWAN PAS DE DEUX*

London in the 'thirties made us feel that here was a dancer with the authentic Russian vigour and attack, and subsequent knowledge proved us to be right.

Among the young dancers in de Basil's company before 1941 were three young men, all of whom became in the next two decades great male dancers. André Eglevsky, born in Moscow 1917, is tall and heavily built, but with his remarkable technique, his elevation and his feline grace he was one of the great classical dancers of his day. His great reputation was built up during the war years in America, and was maintained afterwards with his work with Ballet Theatre and later the New York City Ballet.

Igor Youskevitch's career has followed a similar pattern, and to their great loss, Europe saw little of either Eglevsky or Youskevitch in their prime. Youskevitch (born in Moscow in 1912) came to ballet late. He had been trained as an athlete, and this training stood him in good stead when he first went to Preobrajenska's studio in Paris at the age of eighteen. Two years later he made his début in ballet. He danced leading rôles in many of Massine's works, and notably as a god in *Seventh Symphony*. Tall, dark, with high cheek-

bones which show his Russian ancestry, his dancing has always had great strength and masculine elegance, and he has in addition a quiet indrawn charm, which makes him a perfect partner for his ballerina. He is one of the great classical dancers of his day, and his influence in America on the younger generation of male dancers has been considerable.

The third of the trio who first came to prominence in the de Basil company is George Skibine. Like Eglevsky and Youskevitch, Skibine was born in Russia. He was the son of an actor and dancer in Diaghilev's company, and made his début in 1928 at the age of eighteen in Massine's *Seventh Symphony*. Two years later he became *premier danseur* of the newly formed Ballet Theatre, and in 1942 he left ballet to join the American Army, becoming a Top Sergeant. He returned to Europe, by way of the Normandy landings, in the final years of World War II. After the war, it was some time before he decided to take up dancing again. In a relatively short time he regained not only his former technical proficiency but his position as an important male dancer. In 1947 he returned to Europe, and for eight years he was one of the principal dancers of the de Cuevas company. Skibine possesses what P. W. Manchester has described * as " an honest technique and a simple approach to his rôles." He has never been a virtuoso, but his technique is clean and finished, and fully adequate to the demands made upon it by the purely classical dancing of the *Don Quichotte pas de deux*. His approach to every rôle, and his range is wide, has a compelling sincerity and simplicity. Few dancers in my experience have surpassed Skibine in his ability to portray through his dancing and acting the emotions and character of the rôle he is dancing.

During Skibine's long stay with de Cuevas, the company had a galaxy of dancers which far outshone that of any other touring company. As well as Skibine there were at one time two other outstanding male dancers : Vladimir Skouratoff and Serge Golovine. Born in Paris of Ukrainian parents, Skouratoff was a pupil of Preobrajenska and Boris Kniassef. Entirely Russian both in heritage and training, he possesses great speed and attack and is seen at his best in strong dramatic rôles : in the *Polovtsian Dances* from *Prince Igor* and in John Taras's haunting *Piège de Lumière*. In Skibine's enchanting ballet *Idylle*, a new and gentle Skouratoff was revealed, very unlike the male rôle in Sagan's ballet *Le Rendez-vous*, which brought him international fame in 1958. Since this latter ballet his great promise seems to have been temporarily halted : a dancer, however good he is, needs to remain with one company if he is to find complete fulfilment as an artist.

* In an essay on Skibine in *Dancers and Critics*.

GEORGE SKIBINE AND
ROSELLA HIGHTOWER
IN *DONA INES DE CASTRO*

VLADIMIR SKOURATOFF
IN *ACHILLE*

SERGE
GOLOVINE

Lido

The other male star, Serge Golovine, has so far spent most of his dancing life with only two companies. Born in 1924 of a Russian father and a Breton mother, he was for a short period in 1946 with Lifar's Monte Carlo Ballet before joining the Paris Opéra Ballet. In 1950 he became a member of the de Cuevas Ballet, and eventually its leading male dancer, staying with the company until it was dissolved in 1962. He lives only for dancing, and serves the art of ballet with a

MILORAD MISKOVITCH

companies. Oleg Briansky, born in Brussels in 1929 of Russian parents, made his début with the Ballets des Champs-Elysées in 1947, after training with Katchourowsky, Victor Gsovsky and Boris Kniassef. Like so many other outstanding male dancers of the post-Diaghilev era who have emerged outside Russia, he is, in birth and training, essentially Russian. But he is not obviously Russian in looks or in his dancing. He is tall, slim, and has a fine presence, dark flashing eyes, and a great charm which suggests something of the Latin temperament. His first appearances with the Festival Ballet in 1951 caused a sensation. England certainly had never seen a dancer quite like this, and he immediately captivated his London audiences. His charm and dash, and his fine classical technique were seen to great advantage in such virtuoso demonstrations as the *Don Quichotte pas de deux*. After he left Festival Ballet he appeared as guest artist with various companies, and made a brilliant partner to Toumanova, and later to Beryl Grey in a number of concert tours. He has returned to Festival Ballet and other companies from time to time, but so far has not found a company where he can settle permanently, which is a great loss to ballet and to his own fulfilment as a dancer.

Milorad Miskovitch is another dancer who has found no important permanent company to work with, although he has been fortunate in having for some years a small select company of his own. Born in Yugoslavia in 1928, he studied in Belgrade, and later in Paris with Kniassef and Preobrajenska. He came to the fore when dancing with Roland Petit's Ballets de Paris in 1949, his qualities being specially revealed in William Dollar's *Le Combat*. Periods of ill-health have prevented him from becoming a virtuoso classical dancer, and he has become instead an outstanding exponent in ballets of the modern French school, such as Maurice Béjart's *Prométhée* and Milko Sparemblek's *L'Echelle* and *Quatuor*. In features and physique he looks like a young Greek god, and in purely classical works he has a noble elegance.

* * *

Apart from the dancers of the Royal Danish Ballet already mentioned, there have been few other male dancers from Scandinavia who have made a name on the international stage. One exception is Caj Selling of the Royal Swedish Ballet, who has partnered Beryl Grey with considerable success in The Royal Ballet and elsewhere. Tall and slim, and with fair good looks, he made an excellent foil to the dark beauty of Beryl Grey : his dancing in the classical ballets was clean and precise and he was a partner in the great tradition of *danseurs nobles*.

relentless devotion. After years of intensive training he has become one of the great classical dancers of his generation. Slim and lithe, he has an extraordinary lightness and exceptional elevation. On stage he seems unconscious of his audience, and he never condescends to win their sympathy or approbation, except by the superb quality of his dancing. His range of parts is wide, but it is in rôles which demand virtuosity and the perfection of classical technique that he is supreme, rather than in rôles demanding characterisation. His indrawn personality makes him ideally suited to *Spectre de la Rose* : his soaring leaps, his air of mystery, the sexless nature of his interpretation of the Spirit of the Rose, place him apart, in this writer's experience, from all other dancers of his generation in this rôle.

In the European scene, apart from Russia and England, mention must be made of one or two other dancers of outstanding merit who have not been attached for any length of time to important

JOHN KRIZA IN *FANCY FREE*
WITH ERIC BRAUN AND ENRIQUE MARTINEZ

In America, as in England, national interest in ballet is comparatively recent, and the companies which have been formed there since de Basil crossed the Atlantic in the nineteen-thirties, first had to rely on dancers from other countries. Several have already been mentioned : Eglevsky, Youskevitch and Skibine, and to these must be added Anton Dolin, who for nearly ten years, from 1939 to 1948, was an outstanding personality on the American ballet stage.

One of the first purely American male dancers to emerge was John Kriza. Born of Czech-American parentage in 1919, he studied under Bentley Stone, Antony Tudor and Anton Dolin. He joined the newly formed Ballet Theatre in 1940, and he has remained with that company throughout his career. Indeed, it is difficult to imagine the company without him, so completely has he identified with it his outstanding talents and personality. Though he has never been a virtuoso classical dancer, he has none the less danced in classical ballets with distinction, and he is a superb partner. But his greatest successes have been in dramatic and comedy rôles : in the

name part in *Billy the Kid*, in *Fancy Free*, in *Interplay*
and a score of other ballets. His energy and vitality
are exceptional, and his good humour and
masculine charm, allied to the vigour and precision of his dancing, have made him one of the
most popular dancers of his generation. Kriza
was the first essentially American male dancer
of outstanding quality, and so far he has few
challengers in the special field of character and
comedy dancing. Another dancer of Ballet
Theatre who has earned national fame is Royes
Fernandez.

Two other dancers who have been outstanding
in American Ballet for many years are Nicolas
Magallanes, a Mexican, and Francisco Moncion,
a Dominican. Magallanes, after studying at the
School of American Ballet, danced with various
companies, including the Ballet Russe de Monte
Carlo from 1943 to 1947, before joining the New
York City Ballet, with whom he has been a
principal dancer for many years. His Latin good
looks and his robust elegance make him a striking
figure on the stage, whether he is dancing in
Balanchine's classical ballets or playing parts in
such ballets as Ashton's *Les Illuminations* or Jerome
Robbins' *The Cage*. He has served Balanchine
faithfully and well, and although younger dancers
may now assume the virtuoso rôles, Magallanes

ROYES FERNANDEZ

Walter E. Owen

below : NICOLAS MAGALLANES

remains an outstanding artist and one who has rendered great service to American ballet in its formative years. The same may be said of Francisco Moncion, and in many ways their careers have followed a parallel course. Like Magallanes, he trained at the School of American Ballet, and since 1950 has also been a principal dancer of New York City Ballet. With a fine physique, and what has been called " a smouldering personality," he makes a strong impression on the stage. In Balanchine's *The Prodigal Son* and *Orpheus* and Robbins' *Afternoon of a Faun*, to mention only three widely different rôles, he is magnificent : for although essentially a classical dancer his range of parts seems to have no limits.

If Balanchine ever awards an Order of Merit to the dancers who have served him faithfully and well, Moncion and Magallanes would be among the first to receive them.

In recent years two other remarkable male dancers have emerged from New York City Ballet : Jacques d'Amboise and Edward Villella. There are other dancers now in the company whose promise and achievement is already considerable, and it will be interesting to see if the brilliant coloured dancer Arthur Mitchell, among others, continues to progress as an artist, as well as a dancer. He has a dazzling personality, speed and great repose, a rare quality.

32

Martha Swope

Above : ARTHUR MITCHELL
IN *A MIDSUMMER NIGHT'S DREAM*

Left : JACQUES D'AMBOISE

33

Radford Bascome

ROBERT HELPMANN IN *HAMLET*
WITH ANYA LINDEN AND DAVID BLAIR

*Dominic

The English male dancer has often appeared to be overshadowed by the ballerina. Partly this has been due to the preponderance in The Royal Ballet's repertory of nineteenth-century classics, but contemporary choreographers also have not always served the male sex with fairness. Ashton, in his latest phase, is an exception : the *pas de sept* for seven men which he arranged in *Birthday Offering* in 1956 acknowledged the talents of the male contingent of the company, and the rôles he has since created for Grant, Blair and Nureyev are evidence enough that male dancing is staging a strong recovery.

If we except the solitary figure of Simon Slingsby, who in the late eighteenth century gained fame not only in London but in Paris too, the honour of being the first English male dancer to achieve an international reputation unquestionably belongs to Anton Dolin. His association with the Diaghilev Ballet, and later with Ballet Theatre, has already been mentioned. He also played a distinguished part in the development of ballet in England. The part of Satan in *Job* was created for him when Ninette de Valois first staged that ballet for the Camargo Society, and the four years which he and Markova devoted to the Vic-Wells Ballet during its formative period from 1931 to 1935 were of inestimable value to the company. His partnership with Markova is one of the greatest in the history of ballet. Together they headed the Markova-Dolin Ballet from 1935 to 1938, and after the war they lent their prestige to Festival Ballet, of which Dolin was for many years artistic director. In the early part of his career Dolin was noted for his virile athleticism. Later, it was as a partner, of noble bearing and always scrupulously attentive to the needs of the *danseuse*, that he was especially admired, and his thoughts on that important aspect of male dancing are concisely set out in his book *Pas de Deux*.

When Dolin left the Vic-Wells Ballet his

MICHAEL SOMES IN *DAPHNIS AND CHLOE*

Roger Wood

position as leading male dancer was taken by Robert Helpmann, an Australian, whose forte lay in the interpretation of dramatic or comic rôles rather than in his technique, although he proved himself an excellent partner for Margot Fonteyn during and shortly after the war. His Albrecht in *Giselle* and his Siegfried in *Swan Lake* were competent performances, but his gifts were best brought out in his own ballet *Hamlet*, in which his portrayal of the brooding prince was so intense that some of the other dancers appearing felt afraid of him, and in his unforgettable interpretation of Coppélius in *Coppélia* which developed broader and broader overtones with the passing of time.

A male dancer of a different type was Harold Turner. Born in Manchester in 1909, he studied under Marie Rambert, made his first appearance at the Old Vic in 1930, and joined the Vic-Wells Ballet as a leading soloist in 1935. A dancer with an engaging personality and a technical virtuosity

rare in English male dancers at that time, he will be remembered as the spinning Blue Dancer in Ashton's *Les Patineurs* and the martial Red Knight in de Valois' *Checkmate*. When he retired he became a teacher at the Royal Ballet School and appeared occasionally on the stage in character parts. His sudden death in 1962 was a severe loss to the company : he died in the theatre which was the centre of his life, collapsing at the entrance of his dressing-room after a rehearsal of *The Good-Humoured Ladies*.

Michael Somes, who was Helpmann's successor as Margot Fonteyn's regular partner, was the first male scholarship winner to enter the Sadler's Wells Ballet School. His career was interrupted by the war, but afterwards he emerged as a *danseur noble* of the highest distinction. His technical strength was always controlled, and he served his ballerina with self-effacing concern and became a model of what a partner should be. He was, and is, an artist of great polish. It will

35

Houston Rogers

Left : ALEXANDER GRANT
IN *LA FILLE MAL GARDÉE*

Gordon Anthony

Right : STANLEY HOLDEN
IN *THE PROSPECT BEFORE US*

be a long time before the memory of his performances in *Ballet Imperial*, *Daphnis and Chloe* and *Ondine*, to name only three of his creations, is effaced, and more recently, in his character study of the Father in *Marguerite and Armand*, he gave an object lesson in the art of achieving effect with economy of movement.

The tradition of character dancing is to-day being carried on by Alexander Grant and Stanley Holden. Grant, a New Zealander by birth, is one of the many excellent dancers from the Commonwealth. A product of the Sadler's Wells Ballet School, he had his first great chance when Massine chose him for the part of the Barber in *Mam'zelle Angot* in 1947. Since then many rôles have been created for him, the finest of them, in many people's opinion, being Alain in *La Fille Mal Gardée*, a simpleton who not only arouses laughter but engages our sympathy at the same time. It is in this same ballet that Stanley Holden gives one of his outstanding interpretations, as the Mother, a superb example of character dancing which derives instinctively from the broad humour of the music hall and the pantomime. It is not for nothing that Holden was born in London.

The standard of male dancing in England has risen high since the bleak days of the Second World War. In the classical style, John Gilpin commands an international reputation for the sheer brilliance and finish of his technique.

Gordon Anthony

HAROLD TURNER
IN *THE RAKE'S PROGRESS*

Rambert trained, he entered the Ballet Rambert in 1945, at the early age of fifteen, and caused an immediate sensation by his precocity. In 1950 he joined Festival Ballet, and for that company he created rôles in many ballets—*The Witch Boy* and *Symphony for Fun* being just two—and enjoyed numerous triumphs abroad, and is now its artistic director.

In The Royal Ballet, David Blair now heads the list of English-born male dancers. In the days when dancers were classified according to their build and temperament, he would have been termed a *demi-caractère* dancer rather than a *danseur noble*, and the rôles which suit him best are the heroes of comedy : the supercilious Captain Belleye in *Pineapple Poll* and Colas in *La Fille Mal Gardée*, which brings out his open, smiling personality and allows him to display his virile strength and assurance.

37

Paul Wilson

Left : JOHN GILPIN AND ANITA LANDA
IN *NAPOLI*

DAVID BLAIR *Paul Wilson*
IN *THE SLEEPING BEAUTY*

No review of male dancing would be complete without a mention of that extraordinary personality, Rudolf Nureyev. Not since Nijinsky has a dancer inspired such a cult. The adulation with which Nureyev is greeted by his admirers is almost of the same order as that reserved for top-line variety stars, and it is not easy to assess his genius as an artist with complete detachment. But genius there certainly is, and his appearance with the Kirov Ballet in 1961 and later his association with The Royal Ballet as guest artist have given male dancing a comparatively new perspective. With him Margot Fonteyn has formed a partnership which has inspired her to fresh peaks of artistry ; and with his smouldering performance in *Marguerite and Armand* he has shown that he is more than a dancer of staggering technical prowess, he is an interpretative artist of rare and profound dramatic power.

With the impact of Nureyev to point the lesson, the days when male dancers were scorned now seem very far away, and ballet is only the better for it. Public taste is at last accepting the male dancer in his own right, but it is dangerous to be complacent, for his victory is not yet consolidated. It is up to these dancers themselves and to the choreographers who work for them now to establish their position on an equal level with the ballerinas, and this they must do by cultivating the qualities which have won fame for the great male dancers of the past and the present day. The qualities must vary, of course, with each individual artist. The first, the most personal, and the most essential of all, is personality. A virile masculinity, which is not incompatible with grace and elegance, is also an indispensable asset : much harm has been done to the cause of male dancing by dancers lacking this quality. Then there are the qualities of style, such as nobility, required in the classical rôles, the power to convey feeling, the attack of a brilliant technique, the ability to convey nuances of movement by expressive gesture, and other hallmarks of an individual's execution. There are great prizes to be won in the male dancer's struggle for equality, which will not be won until dancing is regarded as a career for boys as honourable as acting and the supply of male dance students reaches adequate proportions. Much has been gained already, as the efforts of the artists mentioned in these pages bear witness, but it is vital that the importance and prestige of the male dancer be maintained, if ballet is to develop as a healthy, vital art-form.

RUDOLF NUREYEV AND MARGOT FONTEYN
IN *MARGUERITE AND ARMAND*

INDEX